Not Half The Trubles

A Letter From Virginia Reed
May 16, 1847

edited by
Charles H. Dodd

19th Century Publications
1996

This Publication of Virginia Reed's Letter is
made possible through the

Courtesy of the Southwest Museum, Los Angeles, California

From the Virginia Reed Collection, MS543.

∞∞∞∞∞∞∞∞∞∞∞∞∞∞∞∞∞∞∞∞∞∞∞∞∞∞∞∞∞∞∞

Second Printing 2007
(Repagination, insignificant corrections in
editor's notes.)

∞∞∞∞∞∞∞∞∞∞∞∞∞∞∞∞∞∞∞∞∞∞∞∞∞∞∞∞∞∞∞

ISBN 0-9653876-0-7

Virginia E. Reed
(Mrs. J. M. Murphy)
1880

Introduction

Thirteen-year-old Virginia Reed wrote the letter replicated on the following pages to inform a cousin "about the trubels getting to Callifornia."

Those troubles have become notorious in the history of America's overland migration because Virginia was a member of the Donner Party that was trapped in the Sierra Nevada in the heavy snows of the winter of 1846-47. Virginia was one of approximately half of the party who survived to complete their journey. Virginia was also one of those for whom survival did not mean eating the remains of their dead companions.

Virginia's spirit shows powerfully through her writing — it dominates her letter and it leaves us with a dramatic picture of youth determined to embrace life.

❦

Virginia's letter is presented as closely as possible to the way she wrote it. Although preservation of Virginia's spelling, capitalization, and punctuation makes reading the letter difficult for those of us who are accustomed to the modern standardization of our language, that preservation also allows us a more intimate insight into the feelings of a young woman who had just completed a long overland journey capped by a terrible tragedy.

Notes on the letter, including suggestions on how to read it, and on the events Virginia describes are provided following the letter.

Napa Vallie
California
May 16th 1847

My Dear Cousan   May ^{the} 16 1847

I take this oppertunity to write you to let you now that we are all Well at presant and hope this letter may find you all well to My Dear Cousan I am a going to Write to you about our trubels geting to Callifornia; We had good luck til we come to big Sandy thare we lost our best yoak of oxons we come to Brigers Fort & we lost another ox we sold some of our provisions & baut a yoak of Cows & oxen & they pursuaded us to take Hastings cutof over the salt plain thay said it saved 3 Hondred miles, we went that road & we had to go through a long drive of 40 miles With out water or grass Hastings said it was 40 but i think it was 80 miles We traveld a day and night & a nother day and at noon pa went on to see if he Coud find Water, he had not bin gone long till some of the oxen give out and we had to leve the Wagons and take the oxen on to water one of the men staid with us and the others went on with the cattel to water pa was a coming back to us with Water and met the men & thay was about 10 miles from water pa said thay git to water that night and the next day to bring the cattel back for the wagons any bring some Water pa got to us about noon the man that was with us took the horse and went on to water We wated thare thought Thay would come we wated till night and We thought we start and walk to Mr doners wagons that night we took what little water we had and some bread and started pa caried Thomos and all the rest of us walk we got to Donner and thay were all a sleep so we laid down on the ground we spred one shawl down we laid down on it and spred another over us and then put the dogs on top it was the couldes night you most ever saw the wind blew and if it haden bin for the dogs we would have Frosen as soon as it was day we went to Mys Donners she said we could not walk to the Water and if we staid we could ride in thare wagons to the spring so pa went on to the water to see why thay did not bring the cattel when he got thare thare was but one ox and cow thare none of the rest had got to water Mr Donner come out that night with his cattel and braught his Wagons and all of us in we

Staid thare a week and Hunted for our cattel and could not find them so some of the companie took thare oxons and went out and brout in one wagon and cashed the other tow and a grate manie things all but What we could put in one Wagon we had to divied our provisions out to them to get them to carie them We got three yoak with our oxe & cow so we went on that way a while and we got out of provisions and pa had to go on to callifornia for propesions we could not get along that way, in 2 or 3 days after pa left we had to cash our wagon and take Mr. graves wagon and cash some more of our things well we went on that way a while and then we had to get Mr eddies Wagon we went on that way a while and then we had to cash all of our close except a change or 2 and put them in Mr Brins Wagon and Thomos & James rode the other 2 horses and the rest of us had to walk, we went on that way a Whild and we come to a nother long drive of 40 miles and then we went with Mr Donner We had to Walk all the time we was a travling up the trukee river we met that and 2 Indians that we had sent on for propesions to Suter Fort thay had met pa, not fur from Suters Fort he looked very bad he had not ate but 3 times in 7 days

and thes days with out any thing his horse was not
abel to carrie him thay give him a horse and he
went on so we cashed some more of our things all
but what we could pack on one mule and we started
Martha and James road behind the two Indians
it was a raing then in the Vallies and snowing on
the mountains so we went on that way 3 or 4 days
tell we come to the big mountain or the Callifornia
Mountain the snow then was about 3 feet deep
thare was some wagons thare thay said thay had
atempted to cross and could not well we though we
would try it so we started and thay started again
with thare wagons the snow was then up to the
muels side the farther we went up the deeper the
snow got so the wagons could not go so thay packed
thare oxons and started with us carring a child a
piece and driving the oxons in snow up to thare
wast the mule Martha and the Indian was on
was the best one so thay went and broak the road
and that indian was the Pilot so we went on that
way 2 miles and the mules kept faling down in the
snow head formost and the Indian said he could not
find the road we stoped and let the Indian and man
go on to hunt the road thay went on and found the
road to the top of the mountain and come back and

said they thought we could git over if it did not snow any more well the Weman were all so tirder caring there Children that thay could not go over that night so we made a fire and got something to eat & ma spred down a bufalorobe & we all laid down on it & spred somthing over us & ma sit up by the fire & it snowed one foot on top of the bed so we got up in the morning & the snow was so deep we could not go over & we had to go back to the cabin & build more cabins & stay thare all Winter without Pa we had not the first thing to eat Ma maid arangements for some cattel giving 2 for 1 in callifornia we seldom thot of bread for we had not had any since [unreadable] & the cattel was so poor thay could non hadley git up when thay laid down we stoped thare the 4th of November & staid till March and what we had to eat i cant hardley tell you & we had that man & Indians to feed well thay started over a foot and had to come back so thay made snow shoes and started again & it come on a storme & thay had to come back it would snow 10 days before it would stop thay wated tell it stoped & started — again I was a goeing with them & I took sick & could not go — thare was 15 started & thare was 7 got throw 5 Weman & 2 men it come a

Storme and thay lost the road & got out of
provisions & the ones that got throwe had to eat
them that Died not long after thay started we got
out of propesions & had to put Martha at one
cabin James at a nother Thomas at another &
Ma & Elizea & Milt Eliot & I dried up what
littel meat we had and started to see if we could get
across & had to leve the childrin o Mary you may
think that hard to leve theme with strangers & did
not now wether we would see them again or not we
could hardle get a way from them but we told theme
we would bring them Bread & then thay was
willing to stay we went & was out 5 days in the
mountains Eliza giv out & had to go back we went
on a day longer we had to lay by a day & make
snow shows & we went on a while and coud not
find the road so we had to turn back I could go on
verry well while i thout we wer giting along but as
soon as we had to turn back i coud hadley git along
but we got to the cabins that night & I froze one of
my feet verry bad that same night thare was the
worst storme we had that winter & if we had not
come back that night we would never got back we
had nothing to eat but ox hides o Mary I would
cry and wish I had what you all wasted Eliza had

6

go to Mr Graves cabin & we staid at Mr Breen thay had meat all the time & we had to kill littel cash the dog & eat him we ate his entrails and feet & hide & evry thing about him o my Dear Cousin you dont now what trubel is yet a many a time we had on the last thing a cooking and did not now wher the next would come from but there was awl wais some way provided there was 15 in the cabon we was in and half of us had to lay a bed all the time thare was 10 starved to death there we was hadley abel to walk we lived on litle cash a week and after Mr Breen would cook his meat we would take the bones and boil them 3 or 4 days at a time ma went down to the other caben and got half a hide carried it in snow up to her wast it snowed and would cover the cabin all over so we could not git out for 2 or 3 days we would have to cut pieces of the loges in sied to make a fire with I coud hardly eat the hides and had not eat anything 3 days Pa stated out to us with provisions and then came a storme and he could not go he cash his provision and went back on the other side of the bay to get a compania of men and the San Wakien got so hye he could not crose well thay Made up a Compana at Suters Fort and sent out we had not ate any thing

7

for 3 days & we had onely a half a hide and we was
out on top of the cabin and we seen them a coming
O my Dear Cousin you dont now how glad i was
we run and met them one of them we knew we had
traveled with him on the road thay staid thare 3
days to recruet a little so we could go thare was 21
started all of us started and went a piece and
Martha and Thomas give out & so the men had to
take them back ma and Eliza & James & I come on
and o Mary that was the hades thing yet to come
on and leiv them thar did not now but what thay
would starve to Death Martha said well ma if
you never see me again do the best you can the men
said thay could hadly stand it it maid them all cry
but they said it was better for all of us to go on for if
we was to go back we would eat that much more
from them thay give them a littel meat and flore
and took them back and we come on we went over
great hye mountain as strait as stair steps in snow
up to our knees litle James walk the hole way over
all the mountain in snow up to his waist he said
every step he took he was a gitting nigher Pa and
something to eat the Bears took the provision the
men had cashed and we had but very little to eat
when we had traveld 5 days travel we met Pa with

13 men going to the cabins o Mary you do not now
how glad we was to see him we had not seen him
for 6 months we thought we woul never see him
again he heard we was coming and he made some
seet cakes to give us he said he would see Martha
and Thomas the next day he went in tow days
what took us 5 days some of the compana was eating
from them that Died but Thomas & Martha had
not ate any Pa and the men Started with 17 peaple
Hiram G Miller Carried Thomas and Pa carried
Martha and thay wer caught in [unreadable] and
thay had to Stop Two days it Stormed so thay could
not go and the Bears took their provision and thay
weer 4 days without any thing Pa and Hiram and
all the men Started one Donner boys Pa a carring
Martha Hiram caring Thomas and the snow was
up to thare wast and it a snowing so thay could
hadley see the way they raped the children up and
never took them out for 4 days & thay had nothing
to eat in all that time Thomas asked for somthing to
eat once those that thay brought from the cabins
some of them was not able to come and som would
not come Thare was 3 died and the rest eat them
thay was 10 days without any thing to eat but the
Dead Pa braught Thom and pady in to where we

was none of the men was abel to go there feet was froze very bad so they was a nother Compana went and braught them all in thay are all in from the Mountains now but five they was men went out after them and was caught in a storm and had to come back thare is another compana gone thare was half got through that was stoped thare thare was but 2 families that all of them got we was one O Mary I have not wrote you half of the truble we have had but I hav Wrote you anuf to let you now that you dont now what truble is but thank the Good god we have all got throw and the onely family that did not eat human flesh we have left every thing but i dont cair for that we have got throw with our lives but Dont let this letter dishaten anybody and never take no cutofs and hury along as fast as you can

My Dear Cousin
We are all very well pleased with Callifornia partucularly with the climate let it be ever so hot a day thare is all wais cool nights it is a beautiful Country it is mostley in vallies it aut to be a

beautiful Country to pay us for our trubel geting there it is the greatest place for catle and horses you ever saw it would Just suit Charley for he could ride down 3 or 4 horses a day and he could lern to be Bocarro that one who lases cattel the spanards and Indians are the best riders i ever saw thay have a spanish sadel and wodon sturups and great big spurs the wheel of them is 5 inches in diameter and thay could not manage the Callifornia horses witout the spurs thay wont go atol if they cant hear the spurs rattle thay have littel bells to them to make them rattle thay blindfold the horses and then sadel them and git on them and then take the blindfole of and let run and if thay cant sit on thay tie themselves on and let them run as fast as they can and go out to a band of bulluck and throw the reatter on a wild bulluck and but it around the horn of his sadel and he can hold it as long as he wants a nother Indian throws his reatter on its feet and throw them and when thay take the reatter of of them they are very dangerous they will run after you then hook there horses and run after any person thay see thay ride from 80 to 100 miles a day & have some of the spanard have from 6 to 7000 head of horses and from 15 to 16000 head Cattel we are all verry fleshey Ma waies 10040 pon and still a gaing I weight 81 tel Henriet if she wants to get Married for to come to Callifornia she can get a spanyard any time that Eliza is a going to maryie a a spanyard by the name of Armeho and Eliza weighs 10072 We have not saw uncle Cadon yet but we have had 2 letters from him he is well and is a coming here as soon as he can Mary take this letter to uncle Gursham and to all that i know to all of our neighbors and tell Dochter Maniel and every girl i know and let them read it Mary kiss little Sue and Maryann for me and give my best love to all i know to uncle James aunt Lida and all the rest of the famila and to uncle Gursham aunt Percilla and all the Children and to all of our neighbors and to all the girls i know Ma sends her very best love to uncle James aunt Leida and all the rest of the famila and to Uncle Gursham and aunt Percilla all of the Children and to all of our neighbors and to all she knows pa is yerbayan so no more at present

My Dear casons
Virginia Elizabeth B Reed

Notes on Virginia Reed's Letter

Today, we sometimes look back upon nineteenth century modes of expression as "colorful." However, those of us who frequently read nineteenth century manuscripts in their original form have come to comprehend that they can have a richness of expression that brings us closer to the people of that era than to some people today, when so much emphasis is upon a bureaucratic style of expression rather than what is being expressed. Thus, we readers often find ourselves closer to people who wrote in the nineteenth century than to people who write today.

The spelling, capitalization, and punctuation in Virginia Reed's letter are certainly not "standard" in modern terms. Of course, little nineteenth century spelling, capitalization, or punctuation is standard in modern terms. Standardization was not a requirement for most people in those days — anything that was comprehensible was "literate" and was therefore acceptable.

Still, Virginia's letter is difficult for us to read. The following tips and notes are provided to help you figure it out. There are also specific translations of and comments on the more difficult passages. When all else fails, refer to the edited version of the letter that starts on page 43.

Probably the one thing that makes reading Virginia's letter most difficult for us is the lack of punctuation that marks the end of sentences. This is fairly common in nineteenth century manuscripts and most modern publications of nineteenth century writing that attempt to replicate the feel of the original inserts wide spaces to mark the end of sentences. This practice is not followed in this edition of Virginia's letter; the "sentences" are run together without special markings, just as in the original.

Your best approach may be to read through the letter without bothering with these notes. (You probably have already done this.) Your first time through, you will probably be doing well if you can detect points at which "sentences" end. Our advice is to read until it gets confusing then go back and re-read while trying to detect the end of the thought that might be expressed as a modern sentence, and insert your own pauses and transitions.

After you have read through the letter and have determined where sentences should end, you will probably want to go back to try to decipher some of its more mysterious passages.

We have not "corrected" Virginia's spelling. As you read the letter, the primary thing to keep in mind is that the writing is phonetic. It is easier, and often much more rewarding, to read aloud when you are reading letters, diaries, and journals written in the nineteenth century. We feel it will be more rewarding if you read Virginia's letter aloud and we assume you will be able to interpret words that are not too far from current spelling. From reading aloud that you can see that *oppertunity* is "opportunity," that *presant* is "present," *trubels* is "troubles," *bin* is "been," *oxons* are "oxens," *thare* is "there," *yoak* is "yoke," etc. Notice, however, that Virginia wrote *now* for "know," *tow* for "two," *throw* for "through," *any* for "and," *propesions* for "provisions," *raing* for "raining," *snow shows* for "snow shoes," and *flore* for "flour."

Virginia's grammar is quite often wrong by our standards. Virginia wrote *give* instead of "gave" and *walk* for "walked," but we can forgive her for that, because she didn't know our rules.

14

Ignore the capitalization. Most people in the nineteenth century capitalized as they wanted or felt or thought looked good, not according to rules. The first word of sentences are not necessarily capitalized. Also, when we read the handwritten manuscript we cannot always determine whether certain letters, "w" and "c" for example, were written as capitals or as small letters.

Virginia wrote numbers in a wonderful way that had a logic of its own. She wrote *Ma waies 10040 pons* instead of "Ma weighs 140 pounds." *Eliza weighs 10070* instead of "170." The tip here is, again, to read phonetically: read "100 40" pounds and "100 70" pounds.

Virginia wrote *of* for "off." For example, *Hastings cut of* instead of "Hastings cutoff." In one instance, on page 11, she used *of* [off] and *of* [of] together: *take the reatter of of them.* Virginia was not always consistent either: She wrote both *awl wais* and *all wais* for "always," and she wrote *cabon, caben,* and *cabin* for "cabin."

Many of today's words were written as two words in the nineteenth century. Some of those are *a nother* for "another," *with out* for "without," and *a piece* for "apiece."

Some of Virginia's use of words requires explanation because of differences between usage then and now, or because of her attempt to use Spanish words:

cash - Read as "cache." The French word cache was used from the days of the fur trapper, when the trappers had to hide (cache) their furs and supplies to keep them safe from the Indians, other trappers, and animals. Americans of the era typically spelled the word phonetically (cash) rather than as the French (cache). It is "cash" throughout Virginia's letter. No one knows whether the name of "littel cash the dog" was meant to refer to the French word or to the English word.

San Wakien - Read as "San Joaquin" (phonetic spelling of Spanish name).

recruet - Read as "recruit." Recruit was a nineteenth century term for pausing to rest animals and people, to permit them to regain a former state of health and strength.

reatter - Read as "reata" [Spanish] or "riata" [English]. Today we would more typically use "lariat."

Some phrases that might be hard to decipher are:

On page 3: *we met that and 2 Indians*
Read as "we met that man and 2 Indians." Virginia consistently referred to Charles Stanton as "the man" or "that man."

On page 5: *the Weman were all so tirder caring there children*
Read as "the women were all so tired from carrying their children."

On page 5: *cattel was so poor thay could non hadley git up*
Read as "cattle [oxen] were so poor they could not hardly get up."

On page 8: *that was the hades thing yet to come on and leive them thar did not now but what thay would starve*
Read as "that was the hardest thing yet, to come on and leave them there. [We] did not know but what they would starve."

On page 9: *they raped the chidlren up*
Read as "they wrapped the children up."

16

On page 11: *be Bocarro that one who lases cattel*
Read as "be a vaquero, who lassos cattle."

On page 12: *pa is yerbayan*
Read as "Pa is at Yerba Buena [San Francisco]." The settlement known locally as Yerba Buena was officially named San Francisco in January, 1847. Virginia used the older name.

Brief History of the Letter

The history of Virginia Reed's letter is described in
Stewart's *Ordeal by Hunger*, published in 1936 and revised in
1960, and by Frances E. Watkins, in *Masterkey*, Volume 18,
Number 3, May 1944. *Masterkey* is a publication of the
Southwest Museum, Los Angeles, California.

❦

George Stewart speculates that Virginia's letter was
delivered by Edwin Bryant, who was a friend of James Reed's.

The original of Virginia's letter was lost after her death or
she destroyed it shortly before she died. Historians now have
only a photostat of the original with which to work. The
photostat is held by the Southwest Museum.

Two versions of the letter, one probably made by Virginia
herself, are in the McGlashan papers at the Bancroft Library.
Stewart records that McGlashan "maintained a voluminous
correspondence with Virginia."

Before Virginia sent the letter to her cousin, her step-father,
James Reed, made "corrections" and additions to the letter. In
the photostat, many of his corrections obscure what Virginia
herself had written and in at least one instance a passage has
been marked out completely, probably by Virginia herself. (The
passage is that about their eating "littel cash the dog.")

Even without James Reed's alterations, it would be almost
impossible to accurately identify each letter in each word
Virginia had written. Questions of interpretation confront any
editor who tries to transcribe a hand-written manuscript

faithfully, and working with an old manuscript now available only as a photostat makes matters even more complicated.

In early publications of the letter, editors made no attempt to reproduce the letter exactly as Virginia had written it. In the years in which the letter was first published, it was the accepted practice for editors to make extensive editorial changes to the text of letters as well as to correct the spelling, punctuation, etc. In addition, early editors accepted the changes James Reed made as part of the letter.

More recent editions of Virginia's letter have tried to present it exactly as Virginia wrote it. Unfortunately, working with the photostat has opened opportunities for differences in interpretation.

In *Ordeal by Hunger*, George Stewart attempted to recreate the letter "as written" using earlier published versions to resolve questions resulting from the difficulties of interpreting the photostat. In *Covered Wagon Women*, Kenneth Holmes has attempted to re-discover Virginia's words by a closer examination of the photostat. There are differences between George Stewart's interpretation and Kenneth Holmes' interpretation.

As presented here, the letter differs slightly from Holmes' as well as Stewart's interpretation, although it is closer to Holmes'. The differences between this interpretation and Holmes' or Stewart's are slight, and should not detract at all from our enjoyment of the letter. These differences, of course, are of absolutely no significance to our understanding of the events Virginia described.

To this editor's knowledge, the letter has been published previously as follows:

Illinois Journal, Springfield, Illinois, December 16, 1847.

Westways, December, 1934.

Ordeal by Hunger, George R. Stewart, 1936 and 1960.

Overland in 1846, Dale Morgan, Georgetown, California, 1963.

Covered Wagon Women, Diaries & Letters from the Western Trails, 1940-1890, Volume I, *1840-1849*, Kenneth L. Homes, ed. The Arthur H. Clark Company, Glendale, California, 1983.

The Events Described in
Virginia's Letter

The standard work on the Donner Party tragedy is George R. Stewart's *Ordeal by Hunger: The Story of the Donner Party*, which was first published in 1936 and revised in 1960. It is available in paperback as a Bison Book, published by the University of Nebraska Press.

An older but very interesting and useful work on the Donner Party is C. F. McGlashan's *History of the Donner Party, A Tragedy of the Sierra*, first published in 1879. McGlashan based his work on a sizable collection of original materials, including many letters from survivors of the event as well as interviews with many of the survivors. A second edition of McGlashan's work, expanded from the first, was published in 1880, and a paperback edition of that work is currently available from Stanford University Press.

A more recent (and rather controversial) work that focuses on the Breen family is Joseph King, *Winter of Entrapment*, published in 1992 and revised in 1994, by K&K Publications, Lafayette, California.

The description of the tragedy of the Donner Party provided here is intended only to explain and provide a context for the events Virginia describes in her letter. People interested in the full story of the Donner Party should refer to the works listed above.

Virginia Reed, whose name at birth was Virginia Elizabeth Backenstoe, was the oldest child in the James Reed family, which consisted of James Frazier Reed (father, age 46), Margaret Wilson Reed (mother, age 32), Virginia (age 13 when she wrote the letter), Martha J. (Patty or Paddy) Reed (age 8), James Frazier Reed, Jr. (age 5), and Thomas K. Reed (age 3).[1] Virginia was the daughter of Margaret Reed and her first husband, Lloyd C. Backenstoe, and was thus the senior James Reed's step-daughter.

In 1850, three years after writing this letter, Virginia married John M. Murphy, who had come overland to California in the first emigrant party to cross the Sierra Nevada, the Stevens-Townsend-Murphy Party, in 1844. The Murphys lived in the San Jose, California and Virginia died there in 1921, at the age of eighty six.

The emigrants who later became known as the Donner Party[2] were part of the larger overland migration to California in 1846, which had followed the main road to Oregon and California over the great South Pass of the Rocky Mountains, in present-day Wyoming. Near Fort Laramie, the emigrants met some mountain men headed east. From these experienced frontiersmen, they learned of Landsford Hastings's latest explorations.

In 1845 Hastings had written a guide book to Oregon and California, in which he had written that "the most direct route" to California would leave the Oregon Trail at Fort Bridger, "thence bearing west southwest, to the Salt Lake; and thence continuing down to the bay of St. Francisco." When Hastings

---

1. Frequently, the ages of the people involved in the story are difficult to determine; many are approximations.
2. A roster of the Donner Party is provided on page 36.

wrote that passage he had not yet been in the country he described but, as the emigrants of 1846 headed westward from the Missouri River, Hastings was exploring eastward from Sutter's Fort.[3] The mountain men who the emigrants met near Fort Laramie had been with Hastings during his exploration, but they did not all share his enthusiasm for the new route, and many advised the emigrants against taking it.

After they met the mountain men, the emigrants encountered a messenger with a letter from Hastings himself, urging "all California emigrants now on the road" to take what he described as his new, shorter, and better way. On July 19, 1846, twenty wagons left the main emigration and headed southwest, first to Fort Bridger and then to California by the new Hastings Cutoff. These wagons elected George Donner as their leader and were then known as the Donner Party.

The Donner Party was not the only group of emigrants who followed the Hastings Cutoff in 1846. More than 60 wagons safely traveled that route ahead of them, with Hastings leading. But the Donner Party became the most famous, because of their tragedy, most of which they brought upon themselves.

Through the Wasatch

The rugged Wasatch mountains lay between Fort Bridger and the Great Salt Lake. From Fort Bridger, the Donner Party followed the tracks of the wagons Hastings had led until they reached the Weber River. There they found a note from Hastings, warning them about the canyon that lay in front of them. He advised them to camp there and send someone ahead to find him, to get instructions. James Reed, William McCutchen, and Charles Stanton were chosen to find Hastings

---

3. Sutter's Fort is now preserved as a historical park in Sacramento, California.

while the others waited. Five days later Reed returned to report that Hastings had urged them to take a new path through the Wasatch. With Reed's recommendation, the party voted to do as Hastings had urged.

Unfortunately, the new path through the Wasatch required the emigrants to cut a road through brush and trees.[4] Depending upon whose dates are used, it took them either seventeen or twenty-one days to travel thirty-six miles. No matter which dates you use, it was too long.

In her letter, Virginia fails to mention the Donner Party's struggle through the Wasatch even though the time they spent there set them on a course to rendezvous with tragedy. The troubles Virginia describes begin with the Donner Party's crossing of the Salt Lake Desert.

The Salt Desert

There were eighty-seven people in the Donner Party when they reached the Great Salt Lake. On September 3rd, when they started across the desert on the western edge of the Salt Lake, there was one fewer. Luke Halloran, the first of the eighty-seven to die, was buried just south of the lake.

The Hastings Cutoff stretched 65 miles across the Salt Lake Desert. (Hastings had indicated it was 40 miles across that desert; in her letter, Virginia reported an estimate of 80 miles.)

Travel on the salt desert was difficult. For some of the way, the wagons rolled easily on a gravely road or the hard, salt-encrusted surface of the dry lake bed, but most of the way the

---

4. By cutting this new road, the Donner Party made a significant contribution to the settlement of Utah. Mormons used the road when they settled at Salt Lake in 1847 and the years following.

wagon wheels broke through that surface into sand and mud below. James Reed had three wagons, one of which was a large "palace car." All the Reed wagons were heavily laden with family belongings and supplies as were the Donner wagons. The heavier wagons broke through the desert crust sooner than the lighter wagons used by the other emigrants, and their wheels sank deeper.

Once on the desert, the families comprising the Donner Party each traveled at the fastest pace they could reasonably attain, and the wagons became separated. The Reed wagons, being the heaviest, were slowest, and last. After starting early Thursday morning, the first, lightest wagons probably reached the springs on the other side of the desert Friday evening. But the Reeds were still far out in the desert even on Sunday. On the morning of that Sabbath, James Reed decided to ride ahead to find water, to determine how far they had yet to travel, and then decide how to proceed. He left orders with his teamsters to move on as long as his oxen were able, and then unhitch them, leave the wagons, and drive the oxen ahead to water. They would return later for the wagons and for Mrs. Reed and the children.

Reed reached the springs Sunday evening, watered his horse, rested for an hour, and then started back across the desert. On the way, he met his teamsters driving his oxen to water. Then he passed the Donner wagons and finally reached his own in the dawning hours of Monday.

Reed and his family waited all day for his teamsters' return, but Monday evening they started across the desert on foot. It was cold and the children tired quickly. Before they reached the Donner wagons, they lay down on the salt floor of that barren desert, with the children covered by quilts and protected from the cold and wind by their dogs.[5] When they reached the Donner wagons the next morning, Mrs. Donner (Jacob's wife) graciously invited Margaret Reed and the children to ride in their wagon. Jacob had driven his oxen ahead to water and was returning to get the wagon and family.

Reed's teamsters had allowed all his cattle, except one ox and one milk cow, to wander off into the desert, so when the Reed family reached the springs after six days on the crossing, they were in desperate straits. Horses and mules were taken back into the desert to recover as much as they could carry in their huge wagon but they had to abandon their two smaller wagons and many of their supplies and possessions. Reed borrowed two oxen to make a team of three oxen and a cow, but that team could not pull the heavy wagon and its load, so Reed had to distribute most of his supplies among the other wagons in the party. The others refused to carry the goods without the right to share them. Thus the Reeds were reduced to a large wagon with a weak team, and only a share of their provisions.

The Reeds were not alone in their difficulty. The others had lost animals too, and had had to abandon wagons. Food was in short supply for everyone so, as the Donner Party struggled on around the Ruby Mountains and down the Humboldt River, Charles Stanton and William McCutchen were sent ahead to get help from Sutter's Fort.

On the Humboldt

The Humboldt River, which stretches westward across northern Nevada, provided the emigrants with a lifeline of poor water winding through the desert. As they traveled along the Humboldt, Reed had to combine his supplies with William Eddy's, and Eddy's team was hitched to Reed's wagon.

---

5. In her letter, Virginia erroneously indicates that they lay down with the dogs after they reached the Donner wagon.

Then Reed got into a fight and killed John Snyder, a teamster working for the Graves family. Reed was banished from the party and forced to go ahead alone, although one of his teamsters, Walter Herron, joined him when he passed the Donner wagons.[6] A couple of days later, the Reed wagon was abandoned, and the remaining Reed family possessions were transferred to the Graves's wagon. From that point the Reed family was shuffled from one wagon to another — the Eddys, the Breens, and the Donners all assisted.

Indians were now stealing and killing the oxen, mules, and horses that remained to the party. About a hundred animals were lost as the Donner Party traveled along the Humboldt. This, and all the other troubles the emigrants had encountered destroyed what remained of the cooperation that was necessary for survival of the group. The Donner Party dissolved into primitive self-interest; it was every family for itself.

An ailing Belgian named Hardcoop, sixty years of age, was put out of one wagon to walk or die. When he failed to show up in camp one evening, the emigrants who still had horses refused to search for him or allow their horses to be used in a search.

On the Forty Mile Desert, when William Eddy was refused water for one of his children he took the water by force. Jacob Wolfinger, who was thought to be rich, stayed behind as the wagons moved on one day, to cache his goods. The two men who had stayed to help him came into camp later, alone, claiming that Indians had killed him. Later, on his deathbed, one of the men confessed to killing Wolfinger for his money.

---

6. Virginia says "pa had to go on to callifornia for propesions [provisions]."

In the Truckee Meadows

The Humboldt River sinks into the desert about a hundred miles east of the Sierra Nevada and the emigrants had to cross the waterless breadth across the Forty Mile Desert to reach the fresh, good water of the Truckee River. Three days after they reached the Truckee, Charles Stanton rode into camp with two Indians and seven pack mules carrying supplies from Sutter's Fort. William McCutchen, who had ridden ahead with Stanton after the party had crossed the salt desert, had taken sick when they had reached the fort and was unable to return. Stanton brought news as well as supplies. James Reed and Walter Herron were alive, although they had come close to starvation, and were drawing close to the settlement.

The Donner Party, now in the Truckee Meadows (site of today's Reno, Nevada), was finally within reach of the pass across the Sierra Nevada, but there had been snow in the pass when Stanton had crossed it with the Indians and pack mules, and the weather was threatening. Despite that, the emigrants decided to rest. They stayed in the meadows five days.

Of the eighty-seven who had been at Salt Lake, four were now dead: Halloran had died before the salt desert crossing; Snyder had been killed on the Humboldt River, by Reed; Hardcoop had been left behind; and Wolfinger, reportedly, had been killed by Indians. Three were in California: McCutchen, Reed, and Herron. There were two newcomers: Luis and Salvador, the Indians who had helped Stanton bring supplies from Fort Sutter. Thus there were eighty-two people in the Truckee Meadows, but death struck again. William Pike was killed accidentally while he was cleaning a pistol. Ominously, this time Death visited in a deadly cloak of white. Snow fell as they buried Pike.

The Lake

Donner Lake sits at an elevation of about 6000 feet, at the west end of the town of Truckee, California. At first it was called Truckey's Lake but the name was changed by the events that transpired there during the winter of 1846-47.

Beyond the lake, and some 1200 feet above it, lies the pass that had led earlier emigrants to California.[7] When the wagons of the Donner Party reached the lake, the emigrants could look up at the pass and watch winter storm clouds roll across the mountain peaks. Winter storms in the Sierra Nevada drop snow in quantities these farmers from Illinois and Missouri had never experienced. In the winter of 1846-47, the snow piled up to depths that were far beyond their imagination.

The emigrants traveled from the Truckee Meadows to the lake that would bear the Donner name in three groups. The Breens, Dolan, Kesebergs, and the Eddys were in the first group. The Reeds and their teamsters, Stanton, the Indians Luis and Salvador, the Graveses and the Murphys were in the second group. The Donners and their teamsters constituted the third.

The first group reached Donner Lake the evening of October 31st, and tried to take their wagons across the pass the following day. But there was already snow in the pass. They failed and returned to the eastern end of the lake. There the Breen family stayed in a cabin built two years earlier, when 18-

---

7. Although the lake is within the borders of California, for telling the Donner Party story it is convenient to think of the emigrants "reaching California" after they had crossed the Sierra Nevada and reached Sutter's Fort or Johnson's Ranch, about forty miles north of the fort. Therefore, for the remainder of this narrative, "in California" means out of the mountains and snow.

year old Moses Schallenberger had spent the winter of 1844-45 at the lake alone. The others camped nearby.

The second group reached the lake on November 2nd, the day after the first unsuccessful attempt to cross the pass. Again, this time with Stanton and the Indians in the lead, the emigrants tried to cross the pass.[8] Blocked by the snow, they abandoned their wagons, and packed their oxen and mules, but quickly lost the road. Stanton and one of the Indians went ahead to try to find it, and probably got across the summit before they returned for the others.

Virginia wrote "thay went on and found the road to the top of the mountain and come back and said they thought we could git over if it did not snow any more." So the group camped. But it snowed, and they had to return to the lake. "We had to go back to the cabin & build more cabins."

The Breens occupied the Schallenberger cabin and Lewis Keseberg built a lean-to against it for his family. The Eddys and Murphys built a cabin against a large rock a hundred and fifty yards to the west of the Breen cabin. A double cabin (two cabins sharing a common wall) was built about a half mile to the east. The Graves family and Mrs. McCutchen and her year-old daughter shared one half of that cabin, which was commonly called the Graves cabin; the Reeds, their teamsters, Stanton, and possibly the Indians shared the other half. The Donners and their teamsters built shelters near Alder Creek, about seven miles before reaching the lake.

---

8. During this attempt to cross the pass, Virginia rode behind Charles Stanton and her sister Martha (Patty) road behind one of the Indians. Virginia referred to Stanton as "the man" or "that man."

It was November 2nd and eighty-one members of the Donner Party, which now included the two Indians, were trapped at the lake. Three of the party (Reed, McCutchen, and Herron)[9] were safe in California. Five had died before reaching the lake.

At that time, there was food in all the camps although it was not distributed evenly. Some of the oxen had been slaughtered, and others were kept alive for use later. There was also the remainder of the supplies that Stanton and the Indians Luis and Salvador had brought from Sutter's Fort.

Attempts to Escape

On November 12th thirteen men and two women attempted to cross the pass on foot. Some of the men would be leaving wives and children behind, but, when they were gone, there would be fewer people in camp to consume the limited supplies. Their attempt failed, and they returned to the cabins that same day.

On November 21st, twenty-two people (sixteen men and six women) made another attempt to escape. They, too, failed.

On December 16th, seventeen emigrants (ten men, two boys, and five women) attempted to escaped, using fourteen pair of crude snowshoes that Franklin Graves and Charles Stanton had fashioned. One man and one boy turned back the first day, but the others, often identified as the "Forlorn Hope," continued. Beyond the summit they were trapped in a snowstorm that lasted three days. By the time the storm ended,

---

9. Essentially, Herron, who joined in the war with Mexico that was raging when he and Reed reached California, was no longer part of the Donner Party story. However, he remains as one of the numbers that will be cited.

their food was gone and some were dead. The living survived by eating the remains of the dead. Later, when they had reached the Sacramento Valley, William Eddy killed a deer that sustained them for a time, but they still had to resort to consumption of human flesh for survival. Two of the men and all five women reached safety at Johnson's Ranch, North of Sutter's Fort, on January 18th, thirty-two days after they had left the lake.

On January 4th, Mrs. Reed attempted to cross the mountains with Milt Elliott, Virginia, and Eliza Williams. Eliza turned back after the first day; the others after the third.

Relief Parties

Typically, the books on the Donner Party identify four relief parties. In addition to these, however, there were two failed rescue attempts. Charles Stanton's return with Luis and Salvador, and supplies from Sutter's Fort also must be considered a relief effort.

James Reed and William McCutchen[10] attempted a rescue soon after Reed and Herron reached Sutter's Fort on October 28th. After gathering supplies, they left the fort with two Indians on October 31st, but struck heavy snow in Bear Valley and were unable to continue. When they returned, John Sutter asked Reed how many animals had been with the party and, when given the number, determined that the stranded emigrants would be able to survive until relief could reach them in the spring. Reed, of course, had no idea that the party had lost a hundred animals along the Humboldt.

---

10. As indicated previously, McCutchen had gone ahead of the party with Charles Stanton, but was sick and could not return with Stanton, Luis, and Salvador.

hoping to find their children alive and each to be disappointed. Their sons George Foster (age 4) and James Eddy (3) had been alive when Reed and McCutchen left the lake on the 3rd, but were dead by the time their fathers reached there on the 13th, ten days later. Eddy's wife Eleanor and his daughter Margaret (1) had died there the first week of February.

The third relief party took sixteen of the Donner Party to safety; only five now remained in the snow. Eddy and Foster came out with that third relief. Twenty-nine were safe in California. Thirty-seven were dead.

Following the third relief, another abortive effort was made, but failed. Then, the fourth relief party arrived at the lake on March 17th, to find only Lewis Keseberg alive. When Keseberg reached the warmth of California's Central Valley, the final toll stood at 48 alive and 41 dead.

Donner Party Roster

Many of the ages listed are approximations.

____, Antonio. From New Mexico. Age 23. Probably hired to herd loose cattle — died with the Forlorn Hope.

Breen family, from Iowa:

Patrick, husband, age 51 — rescued from Starved Camp with the 3rd relief.

Margaret, wife, age 40 — rescued from Starved Camp with the 3rd relief.

John, age 15 — rescued with 1st relief.

Edward, age 13 — rescued with the 1st relief.

Patrick, Jr., age 11 — rescued from Starved Camp with the 3rd relief.

Simon, age 9 — rescued from Starved Camp with the 3rd relief.

Peter, age 7 — rescued from Starved Camp with the 3rd relief.

James, age 5 — rescued from Starved Camp with the 3rd relief.

Isabella, age 1 — rescued from Starved Camp with the 3rd relief.

Burger, Karl. From Germany. Age 30. Probably a teamster for the Kesebergs — died at lake camp.

Denton, John. From England. Age 28. Traveling with the Donners — died with the 1st relief.

Dolan, Patrick. From Iowa. Age 35 — died with the Forlorn Hope.

Jacob Donner family, from Illinois:[14]

Jacob, husband, age 65 — died at Alder Creek camp.

Elizabeth, wife, age 45 — died at Alder Creek camp.

Solomon Hook, age 14 — rescued with 2nd relief.

William Hook, age 12 — died with 1st relief.

George, age 9 — died at Alder Creek camp.

Mary, age 7 — rescued with 2nd relief.

Isaac, age 5 — died at Starved Camp.

Samuel, age 4 — died at Alder Creek camp.

Lewis, age 3 — died at Alder Creek camp.

George Donner family, from Illinois:[15]

George, husband, age 62 — died at Alder Creek camp.

Tamsen, wife, age 45 — died at Alder Creek camp.

Elitha, age 14 — rescued with 1st relief.

Leanna, age 12 — rescued with 1st relief.

Frances, age 6 — rescued with 3rd relief.

Georgia, age 4 — rescued with 3rd relief.

Eliza, age 3 — rescued with 3rd relief.

---

14. Solomon and William Hook were Elizabeth Donner's children from a former marriage.
15. Elitha and Leanna Donner were George Donner's children from a former marriage.

Eddy family, from Illinois:

> William, husband, age 28 — survived with Forlorn Hope and returned with the 3rd relief.

> Eleanor, wife, age 25 — died at lake camp.

> James, age 3 — died at lake camp.

> Margaret, age 1 — died at lake camp.

Elliott, Milt. From Illinois. Age 28. Reed family teamster — died at lake camp.

Fosdick family, from Illinois;

> Jay, husband, age 23 — died with Forlorn Hope.

> Sarah Graves Fosdick,[16] wife, age 22 — survived with Forlorn Hope.

Foster family, from From Missouri:

> William, husband, age 30 — survived with Forlorn Hope and returned with the 3rd relief.

> Sarah Murphy Foster,[17] wife, age 19 — survived with Forlorn Hope.

> George, age 4 — died at lake camp.

---

16. Sarah Fosdick was the daughter of Franklin and Elizabeth Graves.
17. Sarah Foster was Lavina Murphy's daughter.

Graves family,[18] from Illinois:

Franklin, husband, age 57 — died with Forlorn Hope.

Elizabeth, wife, age 45 — died in Starved Camp.

Mary, age 19 — survived with Forlorn Hope.

William, age 18 — rescued with 1st relief.

Eleanor, age 15 — rescued with 1st relief.

Lovina, age 14 — rescued with 1st relief.

Nancy, age 9 — rescued with 2nd relief.

Jonathan, age 7 — rescued with 2nd relief.

Franklin, Jr., age 5 — died at Starved Camp.

Elizabeth, Jr., age 1 — rescued with 2nd relief.

Halloran, Luke. From Missouri. Age 25. Traveling with the Donners — died at Salt Lake.

Hardkoop, ____. From Ohio. Age 60. Traveling with the Kesebergs — died on Humboldt River.

Herron, Walter. Age 25. One of the Reed teamsters — reached safety with Reed.

James, Noah. Age 20. One of the Donner teamsters — rescued with 1st relief.

Keseberg family, from Germany:

Lewis, husband, age 32 — rescued with 4th relief.

Philippine, wife, age 23 — rescued with 1st relief.

Ada, age 3 — died with 1st relief.

Lewis, Jr., age 1 — died at lake camp.

---

18. Sarah Fosdick, also was a daughter.

Luis. Indian. Took supplies to emigrants with Stanton
— died with Forlorn Hope.

McCutchen family, from Missouri:

William, husband, age 30 — reached safety with Stanton
and returned with 2nd relief.

Amanda, wife, age 30 — survived with Forlorn Hope.

Harriet, age 1 — died at lake camp.

Murphy family,[19] from Missouri:

Lavina, mother, age 37 — died at lake camp.

John Landrum, age 15 — died at lake camp.

Mary, age 15 — rescued with 1st relief.

Lemuel, age 12 —died with Forlorn Hope.

William, age 11 — rescued with 1st relief.

Simon, age 9 — rescued with 3rd relief.

Pike family, from Missouri:

William, husband, age 25 — killed in Truckee Meadows
while cleaning pistol.

Harriet Murphy Pike,[20] wife, age 18 — survived with
Forlorn Hope.

Naomi, age 3 — rescued with 1st relief.

Catherine, age 1 — died at lake camp.

---

19. Sarah Foster and Harriet Pike were Lavina Murphy's daughters.
20. Harriet Pike was Lavina Murphy's daughter.

Reed family, from Illinois:

James, husband, age 46 — reached safety with Herron, after being banished; returned with 2nd relief.

Margaret, wife, age 32 — rescued with 1st relief.

Virginia, age 12 — rescued with 1st relief.

Martha (Patty), age 9 — rescued with 2nd relief.

James, Jr., age 5 — rescued with 1st relief.

Thomas, age 3 — rescued with 2nd relief.

Reinhardt, Joseph. From Germany, age 30. Probably Spitzer's partner — died at Alder Creek camp.

Salvador. Indian. Took supplies to emigrants with Stanton — died with Forlorn Hope.

Shoemaker, Samuel. Age 25. One of the Donner teamsters — died at Alder Creek camp.

Smith, James. Age 25. One of the Reed teamsters — died at Alder Creek camp.

Snyder, John. Age 25. One of the Graves teamsters — killed on Humboldt River by James Reed.

Spitzer, Augustus. From Germany. Age 30. Probably Reinhardt's partner — died at lake camp.

Stanton, Charles. From Illinois. Age 35 — reached safety with McCutchen and returned with supplies, with Luis and Salvador. Died with Forlorn Hope.

Trubode, Jean Baptiste. From New Mexico. Age 16. One of the Donner teamsters — rescued with 3rd relief.

Williams family:

Baylis, brother, age 24, employed by Reed
— died at lake camp.

Eliza, sister, age 31, employed by Reed
— rescued with 1st relief.

Wolfinger family.

Jacob, husband, age 26 — killed on Forty Mile Desert.

Doris, wife, age 19 — rescued with 1st relief.

Virginia Reed's Letter
(Edited)

Napa Valley
California
May 16th 1847

My Dear Cousin

I take this opportunity to write you to let you know that we are all well at present, and hope this letter may find you all well too. My Dear Cousin, I am a going to write to you about our troubles getting to California. We had good luck till we came to [the] Big Sandy. There we lost our best yoke of oxen. We came to Bridger's Fort and we lost another ox. We sold some of our provisions and bought a yoke of cows and oxen, and they persuaded us to take Hastings's cutoff over the salt plain. They said it saved three hundred miles. We went that road and we had to go through a long drive of 40 miles without water or grass. Hastings said it was 40 but I think it was 80 miles. We traveled a day and night and another day and at noon Pa went on to see if he could find water. He had not been gone long till some of the oxen gave out and we had to leave the wagons and take the oxen on to water. One of the men staid with us and the others went on with the cattle to water. Pa was coming back to us with water and met the men. They were about 10 miles from water. Pa said they [would] get to water that night and the next day to [would] bring the cattle back for the wagons and bring some water. Pa got to us about noon. The man that was with us took the horse and went on to water. We waited there [and] thought they would come. We waited till night and [then] we thought we [would] start and walk to Mr. Donner's wagons.

That night we took what little water we had and some bread and started. Pa carried Thomas and all the rest of us walk[ed]. We got to [the] Donner [wagon] and they were all asleep, so we laid down on the ground. We spread one shawl down; we laid down on it and spread another over us and then put the dogs on top. It was the coldest night you most ever saw. The wind blew and, if it hadn't been for the dogs, we would have frozen. As soon as it was day, we went to Mrs. Donner's. She said we could not walk to the water and, if we stayed, we could ride in their wagons to the spring, so Pa went on to the water to see why they did not bring the cattle. When he got there, there was but one ox and cow there. None of the rest had got to water. Mr. Donner come out that night with his cattle and brought his wagons and all of us in. We stayed there a week and hunted for our cattle and could not find them, so some of the company took their oxen and went out and brought in one wagon and cached the other two and a great many things, all but what we could put in one wagon. We had to divide our provisions out to them [others in the party] to get them to carry them [our provisions]. We got three yoke with our ox and cow, so we went on that way a while and [then] we got out of provisions and Pa had to go on to California for provisions. We could not get along that way. In 2 or 3 days after Pa left, we had to cache our wagon and take Mr. Graves's wagon and cache some more of our things. Well, we went on that way a while and then we had to get [in] Mr. Eddies's wagon. We went on that way a while and then we had to cache all of our clothes except a change or two and put them in Mr. Brins [Breen's] wagon, and Thomas and James rode the other 2 horses and the rest of us had to walk. We went on that way a while and we come to another long drive of 40 miles and then we went with Mr Donner. We had to walk all the time we was a traveling up the Truckee River. We met that [man] and 2 Indians that we had sent on for provisions to Sutter's Fort. They had met Pa, not far from Sutter's Fort. He looked very bad. He had not ate but 3 times in 7 days and these [last three] days without anything. His horse was not able to carry him. They gave him a horse and he went on, so we cached some more of our things, all but what we could pack on one mule and we started. Martha and James rode behind the two Indians. It was a raining then in the valleys and [was] snowing on the mountains, so we went on that way 3 or 4 days, till we come to the big mountain or the California Mountain. The snow then was about 3 feet deep. There was some wagons there. They said they had attempted to cross and could not. Well, we though we would try it, so we started and they started again with their wagons. The snow was then up to the mules's side. The farther we went up, the deeper the snow got, so the wagons could not go. So they packed their oxen and started with us, carrying a child apiece and driving the oxen in snow up to their waists. The mule Martha and the Indian was on was the best one so they went and broke the road. That Indian was the pilot, so we went on that way 2 miles and the mules kept falling down in the snow head foremost, and the Indian said he could not find the road. We stopped and let the Indian and man go on to hunt the road. They went on and found the road to the top of the mountain and come back and said they thought we could get over if it did not snow any more. Well, the women were all so tired [from] carrying their children that they could not go over that night, so we made a fire and got something to eat. Ma spread down a buffalo robe and we all laid down on it and spread something over us. Ma sat up by the fire. It snowed one foot on top of the bed, so we got up in the morning and the snow was so deep we could not go over [the mountain] and we had to go back to the cabin and build more cabins and stay there all winter without Pa. We had not the first thing to eat. Ma made arrangements for some cattle, giving 2 for 1 in California. We seldom thought of bread, for we had not had any since [unreadable] and the cattle was so poor they could not hardly get up when they laid down. We stopped there the 4th of November and stayed till March, and what we had to eat I can't hardly tell you, and we had that man and Indians to feed [as] well. They started over afoot and had to come back, so they

45

made snowshoes and started again, and it come on a storm [a storm came] and they had to come back. It would snow 10 days before it would stop. They waited till it stopped and started again. I was a going with them and [but] I took sick and could not go. There was 15 started, and there was 7 got through — 5 women and 2 men. It come a storm and they lost the road and got out of provisions and the ones that got through had to eat them that died. Not long after they started we got out of provisions and had to put Martha at one cabin[,] James at another[, and] Thomas at another. Ma and Eliza and Milt Eliot and I dried up what little meat we had and started to see if we could get across. [We] had to leave the children. O Mary, you may think that hard to leave them with strangers. [We] did not know whether we would see them again or not. We could hardly get away from them, but we told them we would bring them bread and then they was willing to stay. We went and was out 5 days in the mountains. Eliza gave out and had to go back. We went on a day longer [and] we had to lay by a day and make snowshoes and [then] we went on a while and could not find the road, so we had to turn back. I could go on very well while I thought we were getting along [ahead], but as soon as we had to turn back I could hardly get along, but we got to the cabins that night and I froze one of my feet very bad. That same night there was the worst storm we had that winter and, if we had not come back that night, we would never [have] got back. We had nothing to eat but ox hides. O Mary, I would cry and wish I had what you all wasted. Eliza had [to] go to Mr. Graves's cabin and we stayed at Mr. Breen's. They had meat all the time, and we had to kill little Cash the dog and eat him. We ate his entrails and feet and hide and everything about him. O my Dear Cousin, you don't know what trouble is yet. A many a time we had on the last thing a cooking, and did not know where the next would come from. But there was always some way provided. There was 15 in the cabin we were in, and half of us had to lay a bed all the time. There was 10 starved to death there. We was hardly able to walk. We lived on little Cash a week and, after Mr. Breen would cook his [Mr. Breen's] meat, we would take the bones and boil them 3 or 4 days at a time. Ma went down to the other cabin and got half a hide [and] carried it in snow up to her waist. It snowed and would cover the cabin all over, so we could not get out for 2 or 3 days. We would have to cut pieces of the logs inside to make a fire with. I could hardly eat the hides and had not eaten anything [in] 3 days. Pa started out to us with provisions, and then came a storm, and he could not go. He cached his provisions and went back on the other side of the bay to get a company of men. The San Wakien [San Joaquin River] got so high he could not cross. Well, they made up a company at Sutter's Fort and set out. We had not eaten any thing for 3 days, and we had only a half a hide, and we were out on top of the cabin, and we saw them a coming. O my Dear Cousin, you don't know how glad I was. We ran and met them. One of them we knew [because] we had traveled with him on the road. They stayed there 3 days to recruit a little, so we could go. There were 21 [who] started. All of us started and went a piece and [then] Martha and Thomas gave out and so the men had to take them back. Ma and Eliza and James and I came on and, O Mary, that was the hardest thing yet, to come on and leave them there. [We] did not know but what they would starve to death. Martha said, "Well Ma, if you never see me again, do the best you can." The men said they could hardly stand it. It made them all cry, but they said it was better for all of us to go on, for if we were to go back, we would eat that much more from them [who had to stay]. They gave them [Martha and Thomas] a little meat and flour, and took them back and we came on. We went over [a] great high mountain as straight as stair steps in snow up to our knees. Little James walked the whole way over all the mountain in snow up to his waist. He said every step he took he was a getting nearer Pa and something to eat. The bears took the provision the men had cached and we had but very little to eat. When we had traveled 5 days travel, we met Pa with 13 men going to the cabins. O Mary, you do not know how glad we were to see him. We had not seen him for 6 months. We thought we would never see him again. He heard we were coming and he made some sweet cakes to give us. He said he would see Martha and Thomas the next day. He went in two days [the distance] what took us 5 days. Some of the company was eating from them that died, but Thomas and Martha had not eaten any. Pa and the men started with 17 people. Hiram G. Miller carried Thomas and Pa carried Martha, and they were caught in [unreadable] and they had to stop two days. It stormed so they could not go and the bears took their provisions, and they were 4 days without anything. Pa and Hiram and all the men started [with] one [of the] Donner boys. Pa was carrying Martha, Hiram carrying Thomas; and the snow was up to their waist, and it a snowing so they could hardly see the way. They wrapped the children up and never took them out for 4 days, and they had nothing to eat in all that time. Thomas asked for something to eat once. Those that they brought from the cabins — some of them were not able to come and some would not come. There were 3 died and the rest ate them. They were 10 days without any thing to eat but the dead. Pa brought Thomas and Pady in to where we were. None of the men were able to go. Their feet were froze very bad so there was another company went and brought them all in. They are all in from the mountains now but five. There were men went out after them and were caught in a storm and had to come back. There is another company gone. There were half got through that were stopped there [in the mountains]. There were but 2 families that all of them got [through].[21] We were one. O Mary, I have not wrote you half of the trouble we have had, but I have wrote you enough to let you know that you don't know what trouble is. But thank the Good God we have all got through and [we were] the only family that did not eat human

---

21. Here Virginia is saying that, of those who were stopped in the mountains, only half got through alive, and only two families got through intact.

flesh. We have left everything but I don't care for that. We have got through with our lives. Don't let this letter dishearten anybody, and never take no cutoffs and hurry along as fast as you can.

My Dear Cousin

We are all very well pleased with California, particularly with the climate. Let it be ever so hot a day, there is all wais [always] cool nights. It is a beautiful country. It is mostly in valleys. It ought to be a beautiful country to pay us for our trouble getting there. It is the greatest place for cattle and horses you ever saw. It would just suit Charley, for he could ride down 3 or 4 horses a day, and he could learn to be Bocarro [a vaquero], one who lassos cattle. The Spaniards and Indians are the best riders I ever saw. They have a Spanish saddle and wooden stirrup, and great big spurs. The wheel of them is 5 inches in diameter. They could not manage the California horses without the spurs. They [the horses] won't go at all if they can't hear the spurs rattle. They have little bells to them to make them rattle. They [the vaqueros] blindfold the horses and then saddle them and get on them, and then take the blindfold off of [them] and let [them] run. If they can't sit on [them] they tie themselves on and let them run as fast as they can and [they] go out to a band of bullocks and throw the riata [lariat] on a wild bullock and butt it around the horn of his saddle and he can hold it as long as he wants. Another Indian throws his riata on its [the bullock's] feet and throw them and when they take the riata off of them, they are very dangerous. They will run after you, then hook their horses and run after any person they see. They [the vaqueros] ride from 80 to 100 miles a day. Some of the Spaniard[s] have from 6 [6000] to 7000 head of horses and from 15 [15000] to 16000 head [of] cattle. We are all very fleshy. Ma weighs 10040 [140] pounds and [is] still a gaining. I weigh 81. Tell Henriet if she wants to get married for to come to California. She can get a Spaniard any time; that Eliza is a going to marry a Spaniard by the name of Armeho, and Eliza weighs 10072 [172]. We have not saw Uncle Cadon yet, but we have had 2 letters from him. He is well and is a coming here as soon as he can. Mary take this letter to Uncle Gursham and to all that I know, to all of our neighbors, and tell Doctor Maniel and every girl I know, and let them read it. Mary, kiss little Sue and Maryann for me, and give my best love to all I know, to Uncle James, Aunt Lida, and all the rest of the family, and to Uncle Gursham, Aunt Percilla, and all the children, and to all of our neighbors, and to all the girls I know. Ma sends her very best love to Uncle James, Aunt Leida, and all the rest of the family, and to Uncle Gursham and Aunt Percilla, all of the children, and to all of our neighbors, and to all she knows. Pa is at Yerba Buena, so no more at present.

My Dear Cousins
Virginia Elizabeth B. Reed